Time for PHONICS

Marion Ireland

PHONETIC WORD FAMILIES AND BLENDS

HUNTER
EDUCATION
NIGHTINGALE

Copyright © 2018 Marion Ireland
Time for Phonics Book 3

Published by:
Hunter Education Nightingale
ABN: 69 055 798 626
PO Box 547
Warners Bay NSW 2282
Ph: 0417 658 777
email: sales@huntereducationnightingale.com.au
        paul@huntereducationnightingale.com.au
        www.huntereducationnightingale.com.au

Cover Design: Brooke Lewis

National Library of Australia Card No.
and ISBN 978 - 1 - 925787 - 06 - 1
Phonics Series ISBN 978 - 1 - 925787 - 08 - 5

RECYCLING

When the program is completed and the paper no longer wanted, be sure to have it recycled. The time and care taken to recycle may help save a tree and maintain our environment.

About this Book - *and how to get the best out of it.*

- **Directions** in smaller print need to be read aloud to students to give them a clear understanding of what they need to do.

This book encompasses a range of strategies including:

- **A phonic approach** using oral phonemic awareness strategies (80% of words in the English language have a phonic base)

- **Word families** consisting of many simple rhyming words. This base list can be expanded as relevant.

- **Varied, graded activities** that are age appropriate.

- **Core words** - simple common sight words that are also high frequency words essential to all reading matter.

- **Some challenge activities** are incorporated in the mix.

- **Personal Word Box** - words chosen by student and/or teacher, based on student needs. These need to be achievable for individual students.

- **Blends** - consonant blends and special blends are included as they form an essential part of many word families.

- **Syllables** - how to use syllables to decipher new words.

- **Spelling rules** – introduction to the first of a sequence of basic spelling rules, continued in Book 4.

- **Graded sentences** can form the basis for Dictation and show correct usage of list words. These can be modified as needed. Words from each respective word family are used in context. Optional – underline these words; circle phonic blends; highlight word endings etc as relevant to the text and appropriate to student needs.

- **Sentence Construction** - students are encouraged to complete and create some of their own oral and written sentences.

- **Compound words** - an introduction to compound words using known words selected from word families.

- **Homographs and homophones** - a simple introduction using vocabulary that is common usage and in their word families.

- **Revision** is built into the sequence of activities.

- **Assessment tasks** measure progress and can also be used as a diagnostic tool.

Message to Parents

With *Time for Phonics Book 3* you may need and want to help your child with some of the word families introduced to make more complex words. As a parent you can work with your child to ensure the basic fundamentals of learning to read with Phonics. Follow the suggested approach with each sound, blend and sentence and as your child's understanding and competence grows reading skills will grow too.

As your child works through the book your help may be required less. However, ensure your child fully understands the process and outcomes of a phonetic approach to reading. Good spelling and writing will follow.

Praise your child at all times, because you are the ideal support person in your child's life to help with developing a good education. It is essential that your child learns to read. *Time for Phonics 3* will provide a brick in the foundations of learning to read. Work with your child, make the learning process fun and enjoy the journey to becoming a good reader.

and word family

Run *a*, *n* and *d* sounds together to form **and**. Now write **and** in these words and copy. The first one is done for you. Read and spell these words aloud.

band _____   c_____y _____

h____ _____   h____y _____

s____ _____   gr____ _____

l____ _____   st____ _____

It helps to break some words into small chunks.

c+and+le = _____

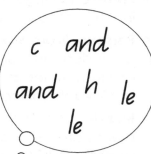

h+and+le = _____

Use phonic blends for these.

th is a special blend.

er is a common word ending.   *e* at the end gives *a* a long sound.

mother   father   name   same

_____ _____   _____ _____

4

Write your *name*: _____

Break these words into small chunks. Use different colours.

grandstand = _____

grandmother = _____

grandfather = _____

Read and spell:

We can stand up to see the band play.

She had candy in her hand when she went to see the band playing.

The band is happy playing in the grandstand. Our grandmother and grandfather are with us.

Personal Words

Run the sounds **a**, **m** and **p** together to form **amp**. Write **amp** in these words. The first one is done for you. Copy each word neatly. Read and spell these words aloud. Draw a line to join the 3 pictures to words that match.

lamp

c_____

r_____

st_____

d_____

cl_____

tr_____

ch_____ion

Circle the words that rhyme in each row. Read and spell them aloud.

camp   can   lamp   stamp   dump   pram

trumpet   tramp   damper   hamper   ham

ramp   damp   champion   clamp   clump

Add **s** to these words and copy them.

lamp__ _____   stamp__ _____   ramp__ _____

bush and **push** are rhyming words.   **picnic** and **comic** are easy to sound.

bush   push   picnic   comic

_____ _____ _____ _____ _____

Add *er* to these *amp* words. Read and spell them aloud.

damp_____   hamp_____   stamp_____

Add *ing* to these words. Read and spell them aloud.

camp_____   tramp_____

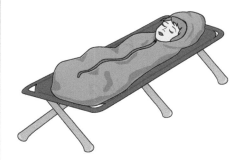

bush+land = _____

camp+bed = _____

Read and spell:

I put a stamp on my letter to mum and dad.

This comic book has four stamps.

It is from my big sister at camp.

Mum made damper to put in my
picnic hamper. Our school is going by bus to
camp in bushland.

Personal Words

ump word family

Run the sounds **u**, **m** and **p** together to form **ump**. Circle the words that say **ump** in this box. Read and spell them aloud.

imp	bump	jump	hump	jumped
bumping	stump	trumpet	pompom	
grumpy	crumpet	jumping	camp	
thump	rump	plump	lamp	pump
dump	thumped	camping	pumping	

Write the missing words to match these pictures.

 a _____    a _____

 a camel with a _____

The girls and boys are _____.

The **o** in these words has a short sound.
The **g** has a soft sound.

very is a sight word.
Phonic clues help.

long   along   song   very

_____ _____ _____ _____

8

Draw a line to join pictures and words.

We are jumping up and down.

The big man is playing a trumpet.

The toy cars are bumping.

Read and spell:

Boys and girls can run and jump at school.

We saw a camel with a hump at the zoo. He was not very plump.

That man likes to play a trumpet in his band. He had to play a very long song.

Personal Words

ang word family

Run the sounds **a, n** and **g** together to form **ang**. Write **ang** in these words. The first one is done for you. Read and spell them aloud.

p_____   f_____

g_____   b_____le

h_____   t_____le

r_____   sl_____

The little children s_____ at school.

The ship's bell r_____. It went cl_____.

We left the ship on a g_____way.

These words have a short **i** sound.   Check the **i** sound in these two words.

give   live   child   children

_____ _____ _____ _____

Circle the words that match the pictures.

a gold ring

a gold bangle

a gold tangle

My balloon sang.

My balloon went bang.

My balloon went clang.

My dog rang the bell.

My dog is in a gang.

My dog has two fangs.

one child

two children

three children

Read and spell:

My dog has two fangs. I give him a pat.

The happy children sang five songs. Give them a clap with your hands.

Give Tess her gold bangle. She is going to a party for children. They will see a big balloon go bang.

Personal Words

Run the sounds **a**, **n** and **k** together to form **ank**. Write **ank** in these words. The first one is done for you. Read and spell them aloud.

bank   s_____   t_____   th_____

dr_____   cl_____   bl_____   pr_____

st_____   t_____er   bl_____et

Label these pictures with **ank** words.

_____   _____   _____

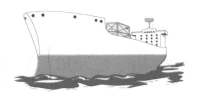

_____   _____   _____

Use phonic clues. Look at the **er** sound.

Look for a special blend and a sight word.

water   *river*   **then**   *they*

_____   _____   _____   _____

Some words have more than one meaning. They are called homographs.

bank

Circle the *ank* words in this box.

sank	sink	prank	thank	blank
clank	plank	neck	cranky	stick
stank	Frank	rank	bank	blanket

Read and spell:

Dad went to the bank to pay for his water tank.

He said thank you to the children as they gave him a toy tanker.

The children sat on a red and white blanket on the river bank. They drank water and had a picnic.

Personal Words

Run the sounds **e**, **n** and **d** together to form **end**. Write **end** in these words. The first one is done for you. Read and spell them aloud.

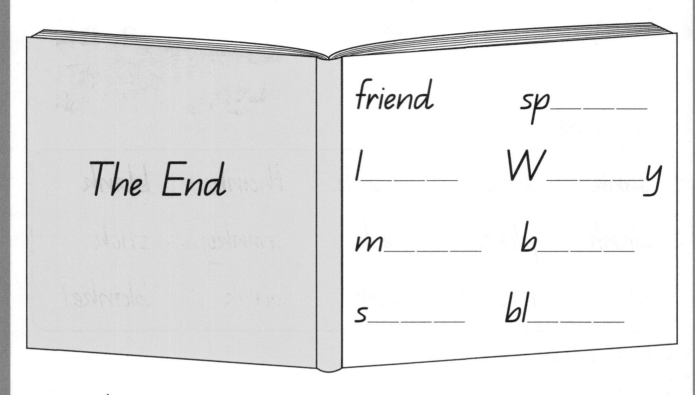

The End

friend   sp_____

l_____   W_____y

m_____   b_____

s_____   bl_____

Write **end** in these words to match the pictures.

A b_____ in the road.

W_____dy is my fri_____. She can m_____ things.

These words all say **ou** which has its own special sound. Practise making the **ou** sound in these words. Read and spell them aloud then copy them.

our   out   about   shout

_____   _____   _____   _____

14

Choose the correct words in these sentences.

When I go to the shops with mum I like to (bend/spend) money.

I (mend/lend) my bike to a (friend/trend).

When I get a (dish/fish) on my fishing line I (shout/about) to my (ten/friend) to have a look at it.

Read and spell:

Send this rug to me. I can mend it.

Wendy can mend my book if you lend it to her. She will give it back.

Give this to my friend, Ben. Do not shout. He can spend it when he is out and about.

Personal Words

est word family

Run the sounds *e*, *s* and *t* together to form *est*. Write *est* in these words. The first one is done for you. Read and spell them aloud.

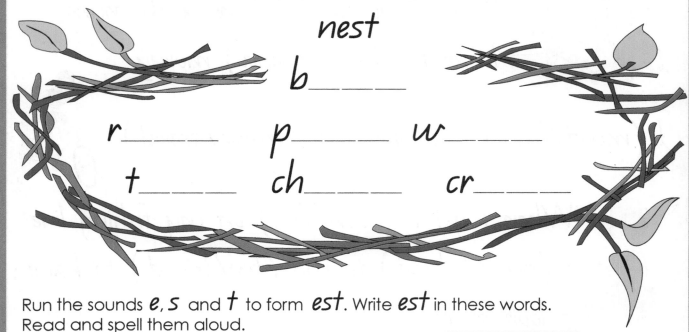

nest

b_____

r_____   p_____   w_____

t_____   ch_____   cr_____

Run the sounds *e*, *s* and *t* to form *est*. Write *est* in these words. Read and spell them aloud.

The sun sets in the _____.

Eggs are in this _____.

I did my _____ in a _____ at school.

Break these words into syllables. The first one is done for you. Spell them aloud.

resting   rest ing

yesterday   ____ ____ ____

interesting   __ ____ ____ ____

yellow   pink   white   bird

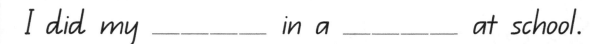

_____ _____ _____ _____

Some words have more than one meaning. *chest* is homograph.

chest

Tick the sentence that matches the picture.

This white bird has a yellow crest.

My bird is pink with a yellow crest.

This bird is in its nest.

This pirate put his hand on his chest.

This pirate has a treasure chest.

This pirate had a rest in a nest.

Read and spell:

I did my best in the test. It was good.

We had a test at school. I put my hand on my chest.

A yellow and white baby bird is fed in its nest. It has a rest at sunset.

Personal Words

ee word family

Run two long **e** sounds together to make **ee**. Write **ee** in these words. The first one is done for you. Read and spell them aloud.

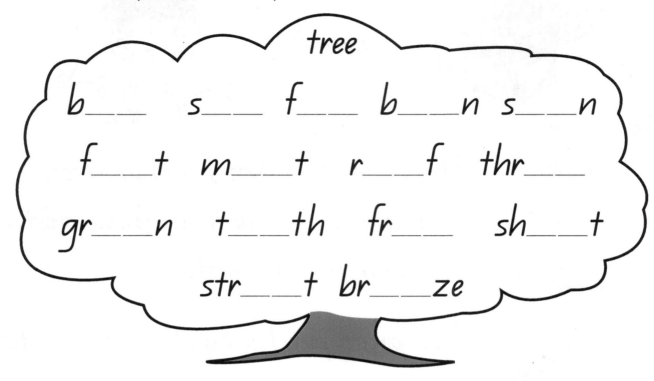

tree

b___ s___ f___ b___n s___n

f___t m___t r___f thr___

gr___n t___th fr___ sh___t

str___t br___ze

Label these pictures with **ee** words.

a _____ on
a _____.

my two f___t

two _____
_____

_____ (teeth)

one gr___n _____

three _____
_____

These are sight words.
The **o** sound is different.

come   **some**

These words have a long **a** sound.

able   **table**

_____ _____ _____

Put a tick next to the sentence that matches the picture.

The dentist helps me to look after my teeth.

The vet helps me to look after my teeth.

Some candy helps me to look after my teeth.

I am able to meet my friend at the table.

I am able to meet my friend at the creek.

I am able to meet my friend in the street.

Read and spell:

Do you have some baby teeth?

Sam put his baby teeth next to the bed in a mug of water.

Some children like to put baby teeth that have come out in a mug of water when they go to bed. Why do they do that?

Personal Words

More **ee** family words

Run two long **e** sounds together to make **ee**. Write **ee** in these words. The first one is done for you. Read and spell them aloud.

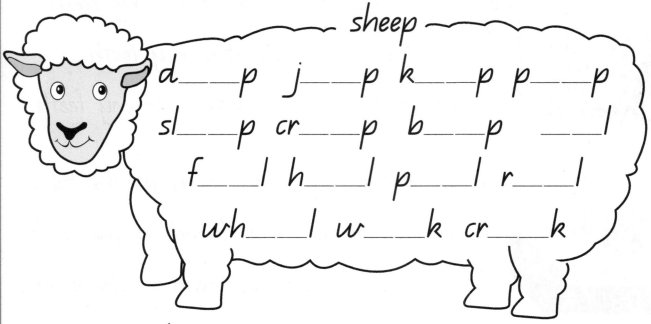

sheep

d_ _ _p   j_ _p   k_ _ _p   p_ _p

sl_ _ _p   cr_ _p   b_ _p   _ _ _l

f_ _ _l   h_ _l   p_ _ _l   r_ _l

wh_ _ _l   w_ _ _k   cr_ _ _k

Copy and add **ed** to these words.

peel _____   wheel _____

Copy and add **ing** to these words.

meet _____   sleep _____

Yes or No?

Do you sleep in a bed?_____   Can a sheep read? _____

Do you have two feet? _____   Can you peel an apple?_____

Do you live in a street? _____   Can you feel a breeze?_____

The letter **o** has a long sound in these words. Sound each word aloud. Read, spell and copy them.

old   cold   hold   told

_____   _____   _____   _____

Write **ee** words on these steps. Put one letter in each box.

Read and spell:

This week we will sleep at the creek.

Three fat sheep went to sleep under one gum tree by the creek.

This week I was told that I need to get four or five wheels for my old jeep to go down our street.

Personal Words

ing word family

Run the sounds *i, n* and **g** together to form **ing**. **g** at the end has a soft sound. Write **ing** in these words. The first one is done for you. Read and spell them aloud.

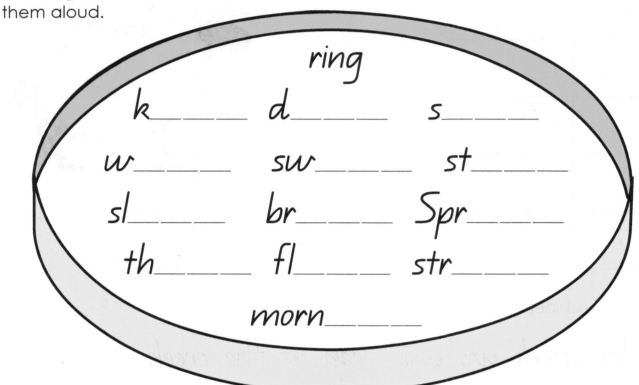

ring

k_____   d_____   s_____

w_____   sw_____   st_____

sl_____   br_____   Spr_____

th_____   fl_____   str_____

morn_____

Label these pictures.

a _____   a _____   a _____

Sound these words. Copy them neatly. Read and spell them aloud.

myself is a compound word.

kept   elf   self   myself

_____   _____   _____   _____

22

Draw a *ring* around the *ing* words in this box.

dong	wing	swing	fling
king	kong	ding	sung
sting	bring	spring	thing
morning	sing	sling	rang
ring	rung	going	playing
in	jumping	doing	string

Read and spell:

The king kept his ring at home this morning.

I go up and down on the swing by myself when I am playing until the bell rings.

In Spring a bird can sing a pretty song in its nest in the morning. I sing to myself when I am happy.

Personal Words

Copy these words and add *ing*. Read and spell them aloud.

send _____

play _____

cry _____

jump _____

rest _____

ring _____

sing _____

read _____

fly _____

help _____

Write one or more sentences using any of the *ing* words in this page.
Add a picture.

_____

_____

_____

_____

_____

_____

_____

Some words sound the same but have different meanings and different spelling. They are called homophones. Choose the correct words to finish these sentences.

to / too / two

We all went _____ the zoo on a school excursion.

I have _____ hands, _____ arms, _____ legs and feet.

That car is going _____ fast.

for / four

The children went _____ a run.

Big animals have _____ legs.

be / bee

This _____ is flying in the garden.

Will you _____ home by five o'clock?

ar has its own special sound when you put **a** and **r** together. Write **ar** in these words. The first one is done for you. Read and spell them aloud.

car

b____   f____   j____   t____   ____m

f____m   f____mer   st____   st____t

sm____t   p____t   p____ty   c____t

ch____t   g____den   ____e   b____n

h____d   milkb____   m____ble

Tick the words that rhyme with **car**.

car	jar	barn
part	tar	star
far	art	smart
farmer	bar	dart
tart	par	ark

Copy these words and add **s**.

star _____

chart _____

arm _____

farm _____

barn _____

What sound does **y** make at the end?

pretty is a sight word.
The **e** has an **i** sound.

happy   puppy   mummy   pretty

_____ _____ _____ _____

26

Write the missing **ar** words in these sentences.

 The sky has lots of pretty _____.

We like to play at a _____.

 The _____ is by his _____.

Read and spell:

Your puppy can go to the farm by car.

Get that jar of yummy jam for mummy.

She will put it in a tart.

The smart farmer has put your drums and four very pretty yellow stars in his car for the garden party.

Personal Words

ar has its own special sound. Add *k*. Write *ark* in these words. The first one is done for you. Read and spell them aloud.

ark b_____   d_____   h_____

l_____   p_____   sp_____

sh_____   m_____   m_____et sp_____ler

Put a tick next to the sentence that matches the picture.

A dog barked at a car in the shop.

A boy barked at a man and his family.

A dog barked at another dog in the park.

We saw a shark on the yellow sand.

We saw a shark in the deep water.

We saw a shark playing in the park.

These are sight words. Use phonic clues. Read and spell them aloud to help you remember.

was   were   only   busy

_____   _____   _____

Put these chunks together to make complete words.

b ark ing = _____   p ark ed = _____

m ark et = _____   d ark est = _____

p ark ing = _____   sp ark ed = _____

sp ark l ed = _____   sp ark l ing = _____

Read and spell:

A big dog is barking at the cars in the park.

Our car is parked in a busy street.
It is market day in the park.

Some mothers and fathers with children were at a busy market. They parked the dark car next to a garden with tall trees.

Personal Words

29

More **Consonant Blends**

Run the sounds **sm sn sw** and **sc** together to form consonant blends. Practise making these sounds aloud. Copy these words and make some of your own.

swim _____

sw_____

snap _____

sn_____

smile _____

sm_____

scan _____

sc_____

sweet _____

sw_____

snow _____

sn_____

small _____

sm_____

scar _____

sc_____

Special Blends at the end of words.

Practise making these sounds and copy the words that end with a special blend.

th moth _____

bath _____

with _____

path _____

sh dish _____

rash _____

wish _____

crash _____

ch lunch _____

match _____

such _____

catch _____

Write the missing blends.

Our mo___er put a fi___ on

a di___ for our lun___.

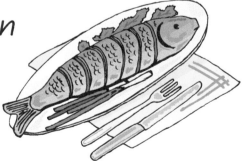

I will ___an this page on the printer next

to my computer.

oo has its own special sound when you put o and o together. Practise making this sound. Write oo in these words. The first one is done for you. Read and spell them aloud.

too   t____th   z____   b____   b____t

r____t   sh____t   m____   m____n   n____n

s____n   d____na   r____m   br____m

c____l   p____l   f____l   t____l   st____l

sch____l   sp____n   sc____ter

after + noon = _____

Label these words to match the pictures.

 the _____

 We swim in a _____ to get _____.

 a _____ and a _____

 The children are going to _____.

Sound these words aloud.

swim   until

Use phonic clues for these sight words.

over   after

_____ _____ _____ _____

Break these words into syllables. The first one is done for you.

remember = re + mem + ber

computer = _____ + _____ + _____

printer = _____ + _____

scooter = _____ + _____

children = _____ + _____

Read and spell these words.

The man in the moon is cool. He is not a fool.

When it is too hot we can cool down in the pool. We soon go for a swim.

After school we like to go on our scooters then swim in the pool. We soon cool down in the water until the moon is over the trees.

Personal Words

ook has its own special sound when you put **o** and **o** and **k** together. Practise making this sound. Write **ook** in these words. The first one is done for you. Read and spell them aloud.

book   c_____   l_____   h_____

t_____   cr_____   ch_____

sh_____   l_____out

Write **ook** in these sentences. Read them aloud and draw a picture to match.

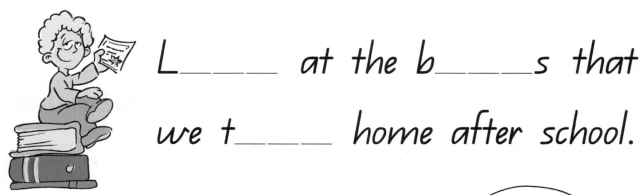

L_____ at the b_____s that we t_____ home after school.

This happy c_____ is c____ing a ch_____.

Sound these words aloud, using the sounds you know. **said** is a sight word

sink   drink   think   said

_____   _____   _____   _____

Circle the correct words to match the pictures.

a drink/brink of silk/milk

dishes/wishes in the think/sink

Read and spell:

Look at that cook. He is cooking a fat chook in a big black pot.

The boys and girls can read the books they took home. "I am glad you are looking after them," said mum.

I said that I think it is good to be able to cook. Your sister and brother can help you cook things for the party this afternoon.

Personal Words

Circle smaller words in these words.

pram	printer	bush	pirate
balloon	thank	friend	white
wheel	been	played	sheep
born	dentist	computer	champion

Write a sentence about a party.

_____

_____

Write these 5 words in alphabetical order.

toy   and   car   zoo   baby

1. _____   2. _____   3. _____

4. _____   5. _____

Put a ring around the words that rhyme with *book*.

look   took   take   hook   hike   chook   shook   cook

Put a ring around the words that rhyme with *school*.

cool   cod   fool   food   tool   stool   steel   pool

Compare the two different *oo* sounds.

Put these words together to make compound words. The first one is done for you.

lap + top = laptop

sun + set = _____

cup + cake = _____

toy + box = _____

zig + zag = _____

see + saw = _____

pen + pal = _____

bed + time = _____

How many words can you make using these 12 letters? Write them in the box.

d   m   a   p   t   u

e   s   r   l   f   o

Do not double the last letter if there is more than one consonant after the short vowel in these words. Write the missing words. The first one is done for you. Read and spell these words aloud.

	Add ed	Add ing	Add er
help	helped	helping	helper
jump	_____	jumping	_____
mend	_____	_____	mender
rest	rested	_____	_____
test	_____	testing	_____
start	_____	_____	starter

Copy these words and add the endings. The first one is done for you.

play	played	playing	player
cool	_____	_____	_____
wheel	_____	_____	_____
open	_____	_____	_____

Copy these words and add est. Read and spell them aloud.

cool _____   deep _____   slow _____

fast _____   hard _____   grand _____

dark _____   long _____   smart _____

Tick the correct words to match each sentence to the right picture.

The children are (helping/hopping) at home.

We are (jogging/jumping) over a skipping rope.

They are (resting/testing) and watching TV.

Read and spell:

The girls and boys helped mum by doing jobs at home.

The children helped mum and dad to do some things at home. They like being helpers.

The children helped at home. They played by jumping about and swinging from the trees when it was cooler. They rested at bedtime.

Personal Words

all word family

all has its own special sound. The letter *a* has a different sound in words that say *all*. Write *all* in the words on the brick wall. The first one is done for you. Read and spell them aloud.

wall

b_____	c_____	f_____	h_____

h_____way	m_____	t_____	st_____

sm_____	t_____er	t_____est

sm_____er	sm_____est

Write *all* words to match each picture.

a _____ boy with a
_____ dog

a red _____ on a

sm_____ w_____ .

These words all end in **er**. *o* has a *u* sound in *other*. Run the sounds together for *silver*.

brother   other   another   silver

_____ _____ _____ _____

Circle the words that rhyme with *ball*. Write them on the big ball.

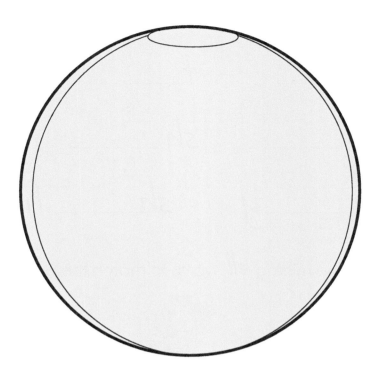

ball	and	call
bull	bill	wall
well	stall	bell
will	fall	fill
hall	fell	small
smell	tall	tell

Read and spell:

Jim hit the white ball. It went over the wall into a tree.

Put the small green and red balls in that other tall box in the hall and call me.

Will you help my small brother look for another ball that went under the cubby this morning? Put it in a box in the hall.

Personal Words

41

Run these sounds together to form the *ell* sound. Write *ell* in these words. The first one is done for you. Read and spell them aloud.

bell

f_____   t_____   s_____

w_____   sh_____   j____y

b____y   sh____fish

Write the missing *ell* words to match the picture.

I _____ over.

I can ring the _____.

I like _____.

I picked up a _____.

Copy these words and add **s**.

bell _____   shell _____

seashell _____

Use phonic clues. **er** ending has its own special sound. **y** at the end of *family* has an **i** sound.

summer   winter   sister   family

_____ _____ _____ _____

A school needs to have a bell. _____

A tortoise has four legs and a shell. _____

A frog has four legs and a shell. _____

This man can sell you the moon. _____

I can tell the time. _____

Read and spell:

I like to ring the bell on a ship. I can spell.

Do you like red or green jelly best? It is good for you in summer.

Please tell all the family to put the pretty shells in the old bush hut. My sister will be able to play with them next summer.

Personal Words

Run the *i* and *double l* sounds together to form the *ill* sound.
Practise reading and spelling the *ill* sounds in the words on this hill.

hill

Bill Jill fill mill

pill sill till still will spill kill

grill frill thrill chill drill skill silly hilly

Write the missing *ill* sounds in these sentences.

J_____ is _____. She is st_____

in bed. Mother w_____ get a

p_____ for her. Do not sp_____

the water, J_____.

I w_____ f_____ the cup and put it on

the s_____.

These words have *st*. Copy them. Make the sounds. Read and spell them aloud.

lost   cost   frost   frosty

_____   _____   _____   _____

Circle the words that end with *er*.

butter	summer	water	whale
silver	another	better	dear
brother	fir	family	sister
ever	drawer	after	over
river	before	never	clever

Read and spell:

Jill and Bill ran down the hill to play with the lost girls and boys.

Will you go and fill four cans of water for your friend? My sister and brother are still at home.

Our brother and sister will help get the water without spilling it. Help us to fill seven tubs as we need them this afternoon.

Personal Words

Rule - Double the last letter before adding *er* or *ing* to words that have a short consonant after a middle vowel. The first one is done for you.

skip	skipper	skipping
run	_____	_____
hop	hopper	_____
slip	_____	_____
swim	_____	_____
stop	stopper	_____
dig	_____	digging
shop	_____	_____
sit	_____	_____

Copy these words. Double the last letter and add *ed*.

skip _____   stop _____

These sight words begin with the special blend *wh*. Copy them neatly. Read and spell them aloud.

who   when   what   where

_____   _____   _____   _____

46

Read these sentences aloud. You can't add *ed* to words like these.

dig   dug

I can **dig** a hole in the sand today.

Yesterday I **dug** a hole in the sand.

run   ran

I will **run** home today.

Yesterday I **ran** home.

swim   swam

I will go for a **swim** today.

Yesterday I **swam** in the pool.

sit   sat

I can **sit** on the step today.

Yesterday I **sat** on the step.

Read and spell:

The boys and girls are running and skipping at school.

They are hopping and jumping and skipping.

Tom slipped over and Jim helped him to get up and start over.

This morning our family went shopping where we think it is very good. We all helped one another and stopped to have a cool drink.

Personal Words

Run the sounds *a*, *c* and *k* together to form the **ack** sound. Write **ack** in these words. The first one is done for you. Read and spell them aloud.

back   bl_____   p_____   p_____et   s_____

st_____   r_____   cr_____   l_____   h_____

J_____   j_____   j_____et   t_____

tr_____   sh_____   sm_____   sn_____

b_____p_____   r_____et

Draw a line from the words to match the pictures.

    a black backpack   a stack of books

    a cracked jug      a packet of chips

    a train track   a blue jacket

    an old shack   a morning snack

These are sight words. Use phonic clues but *aw* sounds like *or* in these words.

saw   draw   paw   jaw

_____   _____   _____   _____

Copy and add *ing* to these words.

Copy and add *ed* to these words.

pack _____

pack _____

tack _____

tack _____

crack _____

crack _____

Read and spell:

Jack can pack his black bag and put it on his back to go to school.

He will pack a small packet of chips and a drink for a snack in his backpack.

He put on a backpack and went with Jack along a bush track. He will draw lots of small birds that we saw at the old shack.

Personal Words

eck word family

Run the sounds **e**, **c** and **k** together to form the **eck** sound. Write **eck** in these words. The first one is done for you. Read and spell them aloud.

d_____		n_____		p_____
	fl_____		ch_____mate	
h_____		h_____le		

Yes or No?

The giraffe has a very long neck. _____

A big ship has a deck. _____

You can play with a deck of cards. _____

A bird can peck with its wings. _____

This is a check pattern. _____

Use your dictionary to find the meaning of the word **fleck**.

The letter **a** has a different sound in these words. It sounds like **ar**. Read and spell these words aloud. Copy them neatly.

last   fast   past   mast

_____ _____ _____ _____

Some words look the same and sound the same but have more than one meaning. They are called **homographs**. Draw a line from these words to match their pictures.

a **deck** of cards

a **deck** on a ship

a blue and white **check** pattern

Our teacher will **check** my book.

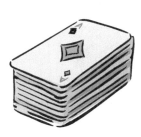

Read and spell:

When it is too hot at home we sit out on the deck to get cool.

Some birds peck at small seeds. Last week I took a book home from school. It was very good to read.

We need to look over our books and check them. Last week my book was about a fast bird with a very long neck pecking at some seeds.

Personal Words

Draw a ring around the *ick* words in the box.

pick	sick	trees	thick	kick
tick	quickly	said	cricket	lick
ticket	stick	stuck	prick	brick
wick	wicket	cork	chick	chicken
trick	tricked	kitten		
pocket	prickly	click		

ick words on this page with 4 letters. _____

_____

ick words on this page with 5 letters. _____

_____

ick words on this page with 6 letters. _____

_____

ick words on this page with 7 letters. _____

_____

Sound these words. *e* has a long sound. Copy them neatly.

begin   began   begun   belong

_____   _____   _____   _____

Copy these words neatly and add *ly*. Read and spell them aloud.

quick _____   prick _____

thick _____   free _____

part _____   safe _____

Read and spell:

A tall girl went to kick the ball. It was her best shot but it went over that brick wall.

One day dad got some tickets for a game of cricket. We saw a player hit the wicket with a very fast ball.

The girls and boys were playing cricket when a very fast ball hit the wicket. Another player ran quickly but he was out. Everyone clapped.

Personal Words

Write **ock** in these words. The first one is done for you. Draw a ring around the words that rhyme with *locket*. Read and spell these words aloud.

frock   p_____et   padd_____   r_____

r_____et   d_____   d_____et   s_____

s_____et   cl_____   sh_____   bl_____

l_____   l_____et   o'cl_____

Label these pictures.

_____ _____ _____ _____

_____ _____ _____

_____

The **g** in orange has a **j** sound. Use phonic clues. *blue* has a tricky ending.

orange   purple   indigo   blue

_____ _____ _____

Tick the sentences that match each picture.

A purple and orange frock is in the shop window.

An orange and indigo frock is in the shop window.

A blue and orange frock is in the shop window.

This pretty locket on the dressing table is orange.

This pretty locket on the dressing table is purple.

This pretty locket on the dressing table is gold.

Read and spell:

Look at the purple wall clock. It goes tick tock all day long.

Jack has a small blue toy clock to give his little brother.
It cost him five dollars. He has the docket in his pocket.

Mum went to the shops to get a pretty purple, orange and blue frock with two pockets for her next party.
She is very happy about it.

Personal Words

Run the **u**, **c** and **k** together to form the **uck** sound. Write **uck** in these words. The first one is done for you. Read and spell them aloud.

truck   b_____   b_____et

d_____   d_____ling   s_____

t_____   st_____   str_____

l_____   l_____y   cl_____   cl_____y

Yes or No?

Can a duckling swim? _____   Can a truck swim? _____

Can a horse buck? _____   Can a hen cluck? _____

Can a bucket tip over? _____   Can you suck a lollipop? _____

Can mother duck lay eggs? _____   Can you fill a bucket? _____

These words all say **or** which has its own special sound. Copy them neatly. Read and spell them aloud.

or   more   horse   story

_____   _____   _____   _____

Draw a ring around a smaller word in each of these words.

horse	fort	port	sort	short
more	morning	snore	snoring	sore
tore	store	pore	wore	core
score	born	corn	storm	cord

Write a sentence about your lucky day.

_____

_____

Read and spell:

Mother read a story book to me. It was about a pet horse and a duck.

Mother Duck took her seven yellow ducklings down to the pond to swim. They all went quack when they hit the cool water.

The farmer took his hungry horse and a black truck to the far paddock. He had to get some small rocks in a blue bucket that frosty morning.

Personal Words

ur word family

When you put **u** and **r** together they make the same sound as **er**. Write **ur** in these words. The first one is done for you. Read and spell them aloud.

fur   c___l   c___ly   s___f   t___f   n____se

p___se   t___n   ret___n   b___n

ch___ch   p___ple   c___ve   p___r

b___r   b___n   g___gle   b___st   h___t

Put a tick next to the sentences that match the pictures.

This baby has curly hair.

This church has a tall spire.

This cat likes to purr.

The tall man is gurgling.

The tall man is burping.

The tall man is surfing.

A purse in the hospital.

A nurse in the hospital.

A curve in the hospital.

The fire is turning.

The fire is burning.

The fire is bursting.

beside   become   became   before

_____ _____ _____ _____

Put these words together to make compound words.

sun+screen = _____

sun+burn = _____

sun+burst = _____

sun+room = _____

sun+down = _____

Read and spell:

A nurse looks after me when I am sick or hurt.

We like to go surfing. We put sunscreen on before we go in the water so that our skin will not burn.

Please turn off the tap before you return the watering can. Put it next to the purple bucket and then you can surf with your friends.

Personal Words

Break these words into two syllables.   Break these words into three syllables.

picnic = _____ + _____   holiday = _____ + _____ + _____

morning = _____ + _____   lollipop = _____ + _____ + _____

silver = _____ + _____   together = _____ + _____ + _____

Write these compound words as two separate words.

spaceship = _____ + _____

waterfall = _____ + _____

sickbay = _____ + _____

Now put these words back together to make compound words.

out + back = _____   Sun + day = _____

after + noon = _____   bed + room = _____

butter + fly = _____   book + mark = _____

sea + shell = _____   web + site = _____

Word Puzzle

x	h	a	p	p	y	b	z	m	s
v	e	r	y	q	l	e	j	u	a
f	r	y	f	e	r	r	y	m	f
d	r	y	s	t	o	r	y	m	e
m	y	e	m	p	t	y	z	y	l
p	u	p	p	y	x	s	x	w	y
p	a	r	t	y	z	o	n	l	y
f	r	o	s	t	y	x	s	k	y
b	y	m	a	n	y	b	u	s	y
f	a	m	i	l	y	b	y	m	y

20 words in this puzzle end with y. See how many you can find. Write them in this space.

_____

_____

_____

_____

61

Assessment Tasks

Write words to match each picture.

90c
_____

_____

_____

_____

_____

Write the correct word in each space.

to/too/two

I have _____ hands.

for/four

My dog has _____ legs.

see/sea

I can _____ a box.

of/off

Turn the tap _____.

weak/week

One _____ has seven days.

sum/some

I ate _____ cheese.

be/bee

A _____ makes honey.

one/won

I _____ a race at school.

Write the name of each colour of the rainbow.

_____

_____

_____

_____

_____

_____

_____

Mark / **20**

Assessment Task

Teacher direction: Say each word once. Read the sentence. Repeat the word.

stand	We stand up in lines.	fall	Don't fall over in your race.
lamp	A lamp gives us light.	spell	We can spell many words.
comic	Do you read comic books?	hill	The children rolled down the hill.
jumped	We jumped over the rope at sport.	skipped	Yesterday I skipped with a rope.
rang	The school bell rang.	who	Who did this?
tank	Dad filled the petrol tank.	please	Remember to say 'please'.
send	Please send me a postcard.	bird	A magpie is a black and white bird.
test	This is a word test.	your	Your hat is on the peg.
keep	Can you keep a secret?	packet	I ate a packet of chips.
morning	The sun rises in the morning.	last	Last night I watched some TV.
party	I went to a birthday party.	quickly	He ran quickly.
dark	It is dark at night.	pretty	I picked some pretty flowers.
spoon	You eat jelly with a spoon.	wheeling	Dad is wheeling a barrow.
took	I took my books home from school.	spaceship	A spaceship goes into space.
playing	I like playing games with my friends.	waterfall	A waterfall is wet.

Mark / 15   **Mark** / 15

Checklist

The student has demonstrated the ability to ...

- ○ confidently relate letter names to their sounds to read and spell simple text

- ○ differentiate between long and short sounds in word families and core words

- ○ understand and apply both long and short sounds when deciphering and writing simple text

- ○ recognise word families where words rhyme and have a common base

- ○ slide sounds together to make common blends such as pl, st, dr, etc

- ○ recognise and apply special blends - th, sh, wh, ch in word families and core words

- ○ build on word families to extend beyond the examples given

- ○ recognise sight words and use phonic clues to help decipher them

- ○ build their own personal word bank

- ○ read simple compound words and create some of their own using known words in word families

- ○ understand and use syllables to decipher words

- ○ use the knowledge and word attack skills learnt through oral and written activities to read and spell new words

- ○ construct one or more readable sentences